Creative Caring

For Men

Creative Caring
FOR MEN

Ideas for men on ways to support and
encourage the women in their lives

Beth Kitzinger & Linda Davies Rockey

SUPPORT PUBLICATIONS / EAST LANSING, MICHIGAN

Copyright © 1996 by Beth Kitzinger and Linda Davies Rockey

Publisher's Cataloging-in-Publication Data
Kitzinger, Beth
Creative Caring For Men: ideas for men on ways to support and encourage the women in their lives
p.   cm.

ISBN 0-9646115-1-1
1.Helping Behavior. 2.Caring. 3.Encouragement. 4.Man-woman relationships.
I. Rockey, Linda Davies, II. Title.
BF637.H4K58 1995   158.24'081—dc20   95-70937

PUBLISHERS DESIGN SERVICE
Project Coordination: Alex Moore
Cover Design: Debra Anton
Text Design: Mary Jo Zazueta

Printed in the United States of America

10 9 8 7 6 5 4 3 2 1

This book is dedicated to the men in our lives who have given us support and encouragement over the years.

Contents

PREFACE

As best friends for the past fifteen years, we know that the actions we have taken to support each other have meant a great deal to us. We often have talked about why it is that supporting, encouraging and nurturing seem to come so naturally to women. The men in our lives may want to support us, but are unsure of what to do.

Having just completed *Creative Caring*, a book with ideas for friends and family to give support and encouragement to those facing life's challenges—it only seemed right to channel our energy towards a *Creative Caring* book for men. This book includes ideas for men on ways they can support and encourage the women in their lives: mothers, sisters, daughters, and partners.

When a friend was reading an early draft of the book, she commented to us: "How pleasant it would be if someone did even <u>one</u> of these. Such a simple act to make one feel loved and important."

Mother

❖

When *your children call for "Mommy,"*
quickly step in and offer your help.   This
lets them know they can count on both
parents.

*If your wife has had a particularly
trying day or week, help the children to
leave little handwritten notes of thanks,
encouragement or just "I love you."*

Identify the parenting strengths that each of you have, then utilize them. Perhaps one of you is the better coach/ teacher or maybe one of you likes to spend hours playing in the park.

*T*ake steps to ensure the safety of the family. Check fire alarms, discuss and practice a fire escape plan, have a car phone for emergencies.

When your wife has a baby, give her a special gift such as the kind of jewelry she likes to wear. Purchase this at least a month before the baby is due.

If you have watched the children in the evening, refrain from telling her that the kids were terrible and cried for her the whole time she was gone.

*B*e the first person to call the florist to order a bouquet after your wife has given birth to your child.

*W*hen you get home from work, take time first to greet and "catch up" with your family. Opening the mail and reading the newspaper can wait until later.

Take time from your schedule to accompany your wife or children to their doctor or dentist appointments. Know the names and phone numbers of their doctors.

*F*ind ways to compliment her, particularly when you know that she might not be feeling the best about her looks.

*T*ake over for the day at home, giving
her the "day off." You will find new
appreciation for her "job" after spending
a day doing what she does.

Keep your things picked up around the house. This is an excellent example to set for the children.

Discuss the possibility of employing a housecleaning service so that this will be one less chore, allowing for more quality time with the family.

Review changes you might make to your home, such as making the basement over into a play area for the children, complete with a Mom's nook for an office/hobby area where she could watch the children.

When you come home from work, step in and begin to share the evening child care and clean up duties.

Sit down together and agree on a plan to cover managing the household chores, errands and tasks.

*I*f you find yourself using phrases like "your daughter" or I can "baby-sit" for a while, you're probably not coming across as an equal parent.

Stay involved with your children enough to know how to care for them. You should know what they eat, where their pajamas are, where extra diapers are kept and proper dosages of their medications.

Pick up dinner and bring it home weekly. Agree on the day with her and <u>just do it</u>. This gives her one evening without having to plan, cook, serve and clean up.

On Friday night, decide which of you will sleep in on the weekend for some much needed "catch-up" sleep. When it's your turn, get up with the children, shut the bedroom door, make the children's breakfast and play quietly with them until she awakens.

31

If your children don't sleep through the night, offer to get up with them on some nights. If you are lucky enough to sleep through this, tell her you really want to help and to awaken you.

Have a scheduled, standing night out every two weeks. Book it in advance with a baby-sitter. Then go out, no matter what.

Be involved with your children. Attend their school functions, make their holiday parties at school, attend parent/teacher conferences.

Read books on child raising along with your partner. Together discuss how you want to raise your children.

*G*ive her a simple shoulder massage—
carrying around a baby or toddler takes
its physical toll.

Help your children select or make gifts and cards to show their appreciation for their mother, especially on important occasions like Mother's Day or her birthday.

If Mom has been up all night with a sick baby, leave a note such as: "Dear Mommy, thank you for staying up with me last night when I didn't feel good. Being cuddled up with you in your rocking chair made me feel better."

If she has chosen to stay home with the children instead of going back to work, be sensitive to her occasional feelings of loneliness, isolation from other adults, and the overwhelming responsibility of being a full-time mother.

Support her ambitions--if she is trying to start a part-time business from the home, encourage her. If she wants to attend an aerobic class, stay with the children while she goes. If she wants to get a degree, help her to achieve it.

Offer to take everyone out for breakfast some morning for a change from the "rush-through-a-bowl-of-cereal" routine. You can all be waited on, the coffee keeps getting poured into your cup, and everyone's day can be "jump-started."

41

Encourage your children to show their appreciation throughout the year by giving cards or writing a note to their mother. Be a role model for them by doing this yourself.

When you're at home, announce to her that the kids are "yours" for the next half-hour. Then <u>watch</u> them.

On Friday night, stop and pick up a bottle of champagne for the two of you and a bottle of sparkling grape juice for the kids. Get out some cheese and crackers and toast to a good upcoming weekend.

Bring in a teenage neighbor once or twice a week to help pick up the house or play with the children while dinner preparations are made. This can reduce a lot of the "just home from work" craziness.

45

If you are separated, continue to help the children shop for birthday and Mother's Day gifts.

Work hard on building and improving your relationship with her. Find new areas of mutual interest other than just the children. Remember, they won't be there forever.

Daughter

❖

Develop interests that the two of you can share. This could be sporting events, trips to the library or walking around the block at night.

Take time to listen to her. Take advantage of the time you have together in the car.

When returning home from a business trip, recognize that you'll need to schedule some "make-up" time with your daughter. Plan to go in late the next morning for work or allow her to stay up when you get home.

B*e involved in what she enjoys. Try to make every parent/teacher conference. Put her events on your calendar and make them a priority.*

*S*hare some of yourself every day, such as feelings, fears or problems at work.

Set aside time to discuss her plans for the week and be sure there is some time for the two of you.

Save whatever you can for her education and discuss the future with her.   Help her understand the joy that planning her future brings to you.

Read to her as often as possible, no matter how old she is.

Take her to your place of work and show her what you do every day.

Acknowledge your daughter's birthday by giving a gift <u>you</u> picked out for her.

*I*nclude her when there are major decisions going on, like a career change or relocation to a new city.

Always discuss your travel plans in advance with her. Help her to understand when you'll be back and how often she will hear from you while you're gone. Leave little notes she can open and read while you're gone.

When your daughter is sick, take your turn and stay home with her. Some very special bonding and nurturing will happen.

Know who your daughter's friends are and support her friendships by allowing play dates, driving them to activities or helping to arrange slumber parties.

*S*how her how much you care by proudly displaying her picture in your office. Keep it updated.

P*raise her for her accomplishments, like completing her school project, a good soccer practice or how she helped the neighbor.*

*R*emember that every good relationship takes two people. You can only get back what you give. Spend quality time with her.

As your daughter gets older, know the appropriate time to be a father and when to be a "buddy."

If you must travel for long periods of time, give her a calendar marked with the days you'll be gone. Young children have trouble understanding long absences.

Fix meals for your daughter. Let her know through your actions that you want to take care of her.

Act responsibly. If you've made a
mistake, apologize as soon as possible.

Let her see you helping with the daily household chores like unloading the dishwasher and unpacking the groceries so she doesn't assume it is "mommy's job."

If you have more than one child, spend time individually with each of them.

Let her see that you have friends, hobbies, and interests. Try not to live your life through your children or your work.

Have your daughter observe you supporting, apologizing to and hugging your wife.

There is a lot of truth to the phrase,

"Actions speak louder than words."

Make sure your daughter will be able to

remember how you <u>acted.</u>

*T*ry not to expect perfection. If you are
a perfectionist, explain this to your
daughter so she will understand some of
your actions. Just ask her to do her best.

*A*s *your daughter grows and needs different limits or discipline, make sure you and your wife are in agreement and consistent in your actions.*

*L*earn to be patient with your family while on vacation. If you're vacationing by car, take time to stop, stretch your legs, and enjoy spontaneous sight-seeing along the way.

While on vacation, drive a car that everyone can comfortably eat, sit and sleep in. Consider renting a van or mobile home.

As your daughter becomes a teenager you will need to be the one to initiate and maintain the closeness of hugging, listening and talking.

Read books such as Raising A Daughter, *by Jeanne Elium and Don Elium, to understand how your relationship is constantly changing with your daughter.*

Your Mother

❖

Give her a call no matter how far away you live. Check on her well being and just ask how her day went.

Show affection. Greet her with a hug, hold her hand and comfort her when needed. We never outgrow the need to be touched. She probably did this for you many times.

Give her a car phone for her peace of mind and yours. Show her how to use it.

Be respectful of her feelings. Allow her to express herself without judgment or criticism. You don't have to agree.

If your mother is single and is uncomfortable with doing her income taxes or caring for legal matters, help her by going with her when she meets with a professional.

After a family dinner, find a quiet corner away from everyone else to linger over a coffee and talk with her.

Give her not only material gifts but, more importantly, your time and attention. Let her know what's "new" with you.

*I*f she is single, suggest a support or social group where she can make friends.

*V*olunteer your services. There probably are things she can't reach, some heavy cleaning to be done or a car that needs washing.

On her birthday, send her flowers to say "thank you" for giving you life.

If possible, take your mother out to lunch at least twice a year.

*E*ncourage your mother to get to know your children. Invite her to their school activities and birthday parties.

*A*sk your mother to record in writing or
on tape her memories of you as a child.

Encourage her to have a hobby or to volunteer her time. Give her the confidence to know that she has the skills and ability to make a difference.

Sister

❖

Keep up with her even if many miles separate you. Make plans to get together every few years if possible.

*A*ccept her decisions. Listen and be
ready to help if asked.

When the family is together during a holiday, take some time to visit just with her. Get away for a breakfast or lunch without the rest of the family.

Call her on her birthday.

If she has children, offer to baby-sit for a few hours to give her a break.

Surprise her by sending flowers or candy on her birthday and Valentine's Day.

Compliment her on her choice of clothes, career or mothering skills.

Share the responsibility for family gatherings or holidays. Make food and help clean up. This sets a good example for your children.

If your sister is having problems with her marriage, offer to talk with your brother-in-law if you both agree this might help.

*A*cknowledge the ways she helped you
while you were growing up.

*T*ake responsibility for your parents'
needs. Don't expect the "girls" in the
family to do it all.

If your sister is going through a crisis, offer to listen and help if you can.

Partner

❖

Understand and acknowledge the differences that each of you have. Capitalize on them and become a team working toward common long term goals.

*M*ake *time every day to talk, listen and share feelings.*

*R*ead Men are from Mars, Women are from Venus, *by John Gray, so that you're more aware of and sensitive to the inherent differences the two of you have.*

Sit down together and make plans for everything from paying the bills to planning the next vacation.

Be aware of other burdens your partner might be carrying. Is she checking up daily on your widowed mother? Is she concerned about her best friend who is going through a divorce?

*D*on't wait to be asked to help. Look around the house and see what needs to be done, such as picking up yesterday's newspaper, setting the dinner table or unloading the dishwasher.

Never forget her birthday or other special occasions. If this is a problem for you, "protect" yourself by buying cards/gifts ahead and keeping them stashed for that day. Mark these special occasions on your calendar above all work-related appointments.

If she enjoys reading or sewing, work with her to find time every day to enjoy her hobby. Help her set aside a specific time for it and keep the children occupied.

Encourage her to exercise to relieve stress. Let her decide on the days and do your part to make sure she has time.

P*lan and prepare at least one meal a week. Even a very simple meal, will be a welcome relief, especially on her busiest day.*

Take the responsibility for sending gifts and cards to your relatives.

*L*et people hear how proud you are of her accomplishments. Tell her as well.

Be careful not to "just" acknowledge the once-a-year events like your anniversary. This shouldn't be the only time you take her out to dinner or bring her flowers.

When going on vacation, help by loading and packing the car a day ahead of time to reduce the last-minute-preparation stress.

At social gatherings such as parties or church, be sure to involve your wife in the conversation.

When picking out gifts for her, remember it is the thought that counts. An item that she has mentioned she wanted, which you took time to remember and purchase, will mean more than an expensive gift she didn't want.

Together discuss your short term and long term budget and financial goals.

*T*ake a few moments to write her a note
on how she has changed your life.

*W*omen *want and need romance.*
Romance includes listening, planning
"dates," lots of hugs, shoulder rubs,
calls and cards. Sex and romance are
not the same thing.

If you enjoy hunting, golfing or other sports which she doesn't choose to accompany you on, then encourage her to pursue her own interests.

Try a new activity together. Sign up for joint lessons for something you've never done together like tennis or ballroom dancing.

When you have made a mistake, say you're sorry in person. Then follow it up with a special evening out. Be creative.

*E*ncourage her to take a community college course she has been talking about for a while.

Join a health club with her. It will make both of you feel better and is an activity that may be done together.

Continue to discuss your feelings regarding partnership after you are married.   All good partnerships need nurturing to grow.

If you think your relationship needs to be improved, suggest counseling or a weekend marriage workshop. Taking the first step shows her how much you care.

Always be honest! Relationships won't last when the trust has been taken away.

Take twilight walks together as a pleasant way to end the day, enjoy the outdoors and have some dedicated time together.

If you haven't learned to cook, ask your wife or mother to teach you a few easy meals.   Consider taking a cooking class.

Ask friends or relatives to take the children for an evening, then rent a good movie and make popcorn. Relaxing in your home without little voices and interruptions can be very special.

If your wife has a chronic illness, be aware of the times she needs extra help. This might include taking over household duties or letting her get extra sleep.

If she is too ill to eat, take on the responsibility for meal planning, preparation and cleanup. Do it with a smile.

If your wife requires hospitalization, contact friends and relatives and let them know what they can do to help, including visiting with her.

*T*ry to understand how important her friendships are to her and that they must be maintained. This may mean long distance phone bills.

If your wife is involved in a charity, support group, or other volunteer efforts, be supportive of her efforts. Attend the fund-raiser, pitch in and help 110%.

When you know she has had a tough day, fix a bubble bath, light candles and turn on her favorite music. Escort her into the bathroom and insist that she not come out for thirty minutes.

Bring flowers for no reason. They are very reasonably priced these days and can be purchased in convenience stores, grocery stores or from a street vendor.

*H*ave you noticed that she's not doing some things that she used to do, like working out, playing the piano or gardening? Help her to find ways to still have time for herself and her interests.

Write her a love letter in your own handwriting.

If you're awake first, make the coffee and have its wonderful aroma in the air when she awakens.

Is there something special she collects? Antique kitchen tools? Ice cream memorabilia? If so, add to her collection when you see something she doesn't have. Better yet, give her some money and send her out browsing for the afternoon.

154

Get her a gift certificate for a massage.

Supporting Yourself

❖

Make the effort to be the best person you can by eating healthy, exercising, reading, and loving those who are important to you.

Take a few moments to think what your life would be like without these women in your life. With that thought, begin trying these ideas today.

"Enjoy life, this is not a dress rehearsal."